# *Unseen Encounters: Angels, Phantoms, and UFOs on U.S. Radars: Characteristics of Trackable Radar Angels*

## T. H. Roelofs
## Alfred Steber

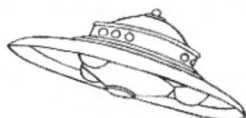

SAUCERIAN PUBLISHER
Original Sources in Ufology

**ISBN: 978-1-955087-67-4**

9  781955  087674

© 2024, Saucerian Publisher

# INTRODUCTION

Radar angels appear on radar screens when there's a recurring structure within the radar's view that is approximately equal to the wavelength of the signal. The angel seems to be a massive object on the screen, often spanning miles, which can hide actual targets. These were initially observed in the 1940s and became the subject of significant research in the 1950s.

In the 1930s, the UK Air Ministry covertly established a network of radar stations along England's eastern shore to create a basic yet efficient early warning system for air attacks. In 1940, during the Battle of Britain, this "secret weapon" provided the RAF with an essential tactical edge against the stronger Luftwaffe. However, despite British radar being the most advanced globally at that time, it was not infallible, as shown by a number of unusual events the next year.

On the night of 20 March 1941, with the danger of German invasion still present, RAF Fighter Command was put on high alert after its radar system detected an assault on Britain's southern coastline. As many as five distinct stations could "detect" a large array of blips gradually traversing the channel, exactly as would be anticipated if a significant nighttime attack by German bombers was approaching. As pressure mounted, the signals neared from the angle of the Cherbourg peninsula in France, reaching within 40 miles of the Dorset shoreline. At RAF Worth, they focused on the radar display for two hours, during which the signals shifted from clustered groups to individual pings, which subsequently diminished.

The following evening, the blips returned, prompting engineers to be summoned for modifications that could remove "noise" from the system. For several weeks, stations kept reporting both large formations and individual signals. Although doubtful, senior officers started to worry that these might be elements of a complex German scheme to disrupt British radar with deceptive signals, simulating aircraft or towed gliders ready for an actual invasion. RAF fighters guided by ground radar were instructed to intercept and eliminate the unidentified objects. However, when they reached the location in the English Channel where the echoes appeared on radar, nothing was visible.

Sixty years after the event, Sir Edward Fennessey, who oversaw the radar system, remembered that no answers were ever discovered "and since we were preoccupied with wartime efforts, we dedicated no time to examining this phenomenon." Later, he recounted the tale at a dinner gathering, captivating his audience with his belief that the echoes were actually guardian angels, "the spirits of British soldiers who died in France throughout the years coming back to protect their nation."

Even though it was meant to be humorous, Sir Edward's story captivated the interest of active airmen who observed "ghosts" on their radar displays. As stated by the Oxford English Dictionary, starting in 1947, the word "angels" frequently referred to "unexplainable echoes" observed not just on radar images in Britain, but globally as well. Since the war angels were noted on various ground radars functioning on the short 10cm and 25cm wavelengths. One source indicates that they frequently entirely obscured the screen and "manifested as a cloud of responses quite akin to the echoes produced by small aircraft," just as they did in 1941. When they showed up as a single echo, they could readily be confused with a fighter aircraft since they maintained a consistent path and were tracked at altitudes ranging from 2 to 10,000 feet.

Angels were still observed in the 1950s following the introduction of MTI (moving target indicator) radars, designed to reduce the "noise" and ground clutter that affected earlier systems. By 1954, when advanced Type 80 radars were set up at the radar research facility in Malvern, angels had turned into a significant danger for fighter controllers. The Type 80 had a significantly superior range and performance compared to wartime radar, yet it still faced issues with angels. At times, they contaminated radar displays to such a degree that it disrupted RAF training activities. At that moment, nobody possessed a satisfactory explanation for the phenomenon, but two rival theories existed. The initial explanation was that radar angels occurred due to temperature inversions in the lower atmosphere, which formed air pockets that reflected radar waves. However, this alone could not completely explain how the echoes traveled contrary to the dominant winds or exceeded the recorded wind speeds.

The alternate theory suggested that angels were actually flocks of birds traveling to and from their nesting sites during their yearly migrations. However, ornithologists utilizing radar to examine bird migrations faced significant challenges in convincing the RAF to regard this theory seriously. High-ranking officials were reluctant to concede that tiny creatures like birds could interfere with their operations. Soon, events would demonstrate their errors. When investigations were conducted, a wealth of anecdotal evidence from radar personnel emerged, reinforcing the bird theory. Throughout the war, operators at coastal radar stations had even associated "angels" displayed on their screens with sightings of seabirds visible to the naked eye. In infrequent instances, sizable birds alone might create greater disorder. Barry Huddart, stationed at HQ Fighter Command in 1957, remembered an event "when fighters were dispatched to track an anomaly on a radar display that ended up being a Golden Eagle soaring at 25,000 ft in a jet stream, quite rare yet indeed accurate."

By February of that year, HQ Fighter Command was so troubled by the issue that it mandated a covert inquiry into angels by its Research Branch. The two-year investigation aimed to merge the talents of its leading radar specialists with the knowledge of British bird experts. Certain RAF radar stations along the east coast were requested to provide 35 mm film from their radar cameras that had recorded angels for detailed examination. Films and recordings surged in, and as trends developed from the information, scientists monitored screens to map the density and spread of "angels" as they manifested. The inquiry swiftly dismissed the "temperature inversion" hypothesis as the probable cause for all except the most unusual angel sightings.

In the meantime, unsettling experiments were

conducted to assess the echoing regions of different bird species. Deceased animals were collected from bird sanctuaries and their bodies wrapped in cellophane before being spun while radar was directed at them to assess their "echoing area." This was found to be approximately one hundredth of a square metre –comparable to that of a bag holding a pound of water! The "temperature inversion" theory is considered the most probable explanation for nearly all angel sighting reports, except for the most extraordinary ones.

By 1958, the focus of the investigation shifted to a primary radar station where sightings of angels had been frequently reported. RAF Trimingham, located close to Cromer on the Norfolk coastline, was among the initial sites to be fitted with the Type 80 radar. Ornithologist David Lack utilized this as a foundation to perform spot checks for angel echoes six times daily over a period of eleven months. This indicated that the most intense angel activity took place in the spring and autumn months, typically at night in calm weather when birds were migrating over the ocean at altitudes ranging from 2,000 to 4,000 feet. Lack and his team successfully showed that the radars were actually detecting groups of small birds migrating to and from East Anglia and Continental Europe. He discovered that autumn was the prime season as skylarks, chaffinches, and starlings came in vast quantities. The second major movement started in late February as the same species left, aligning with the peak periods for angel activity.

Additional independent evidence emerged in 1959 when personnel utilizing Marconi's experimental L-band radar at Chelmsford in Essex noted peculiar "ring angels" on their displays. These started at dawn as a dot echo and then broadened into a perfect circle, succeeded by additional concentric circles that had "exactly the same look as the ripples on a pond spreading from a point of disturbance." The ripples could be seen up to a height of 2,000 feet, and it was believed they could have resulted from warm air pockets rising from factory or mill chimneys. Nevertheless, when teams were dispatched to locate the source of the rings, all they could see was open countryside. It was then observed that a cluster of trees seemed to be filled with starlings. As the researchers observed, at dawn's arrival, a flock of birds abruptly and quietly departed from the trees in uniform directions before reaching another outer ring of trees. From that point, they flew off once more as if reacting to a hidden signal. These findings, combined with Fighter Command's research, prompted the RAF to determine that most "angel" echoes on radar resulted from birds.

However, a significant issue persisted. How could "angels" be removed from radar without disrupting the tracking and management of military planes? The response was a device known as 'Swept Gain' or Sensitivity Time Control (STC). This naturally decreased the visibility of constant echoes in the radar display and enhanced the intensity of those produced by aircraft. For angels, it was an easy procedure to adjust the swept gain controls, ensuring that the 0.01 sq metre echoing zones of birds were automatically eliminated from the radar display, thus allowing the one square metre aircraft targets to remain distinctly visible. This became even more straightforward when airplanes were equipped with transponders that send an identification signal to ground radar.

In the 1960s, radar technology advanced rapidly as stronger systems were created to manage the continual rise in air traffic. Digital computers were subsequently enlisted to manage the intricate job of concurrently monitoring numerous aircraft of various shapes and sizes. To distinguish the important signals from the unnecessary noise cluttering air traffic control screens, modern technology automatically eliminates noise caused by weather systems, birds, insects, and other "false echoes," including those potentially generated by actual UFOs (whatever those may be) right at the source. This clarifies why most radar UFO sightings were reported in the 1940s and 1950s, prior to advancements in radar and computer technology that removed them from contemporary devices.

In its early history, radar was plagued by technical issues that frequently resulted in dramatic interpretations of "angels" as hostile planes and UFOs. A common misunderstanding is that radar, similar to a camera, cannot be deceptive and that UFOs "verified" by radar must, by definition, be tangible mechanical objects potentially from outer space.

This title is an authentic reproduction of the original technical manual:*Characteristics of Trackable Radar Angels*, Scientific Report No. 2 (RSR REPORT NO. **137** Project 8622, TASK 86222, Contract No. AF19(604)-6160) by T. H. Roelofs. Center for Radiophysics and Space Research, CORNELL UNIVERSITY, Ithaca, New York. Prepared for Geophysics Research Directorate, Air Force

Cambridge Research Laboratories, Office of Aerospace Research, United States Air Force, Bedford, Massachusetts on January 16, 1963.

*This study concluded that: A careful examination of the horizontal and vertical angel motions has shown that these targets are undoubtedly windborne. This completely eliminates the possibility of birds, large insects or any flying thing as an explanation for these targets. A flying target would have to show an appreciable speed relative to the wind in order to maintain altitude.*

However, witnesses indicate that the speed of unidentified flying objects (UFOs) differs significantly according to various reports and sightings. Certain witnesses assert they have observed UFOs traveling at astonishing velocities, frequently surpassing 1,000 miles per hour (1,609 kilometers per hour) or even considerably more. For example, in military documents, certain UFOs have been depicted as executing swift movements that challenge standard aerodynamics, indicating speeds that may reach supersonic or hypersonic levels.

**IMPORTANT.** Because this material is culturally important, we have made it available as part of our commitment to protect, preserve, and promote knowledge in the world.

# TABLE OF CONTENTS

## ACKNOWLEDGEMENTS

The author gratefully acknowledges the contributions to this report by D. B. Rai and R. Bolgiano, Jr.

Sincere thanks are due to personnel of the National Aeronautics and Space Administration at Wallops Station. The collection of data was made-possible by their splendid assistance and cooperation.

# CHARACTERISTICS OF TRACKABLE RADAR ANGELS

## Abstract

Clear air radar angels were tracked with an FPS-16 radar at Wallops Island, Virginia. Observations were made at different times of the year under a variety of weather conditions. On cloudy days, echoes having characteristics similar to clear air angels were tracked.

The radar had a beam width of 1.2 degree; a wavelength of 5.5 centimeters, and was operated at a pulse length of 0.25 microsecond with a peak power of 1.2 megawatts.

Data consist of flight trajectories of the echoes and a record of power returned. Radiosonde profiles of the atmosphere were obtained from an on-site weather station.

It may be that this kind of data can not only clarify the angel problem but also provide convenient means for studying local atmospheric motions, such as the sea breeze.

Evidence is given that indicates the meteorological nature of angels. A tentative model is suggested which would account for most of the observed characteristics.

# INTRODUCTION

Generally speaking radar "angels" may be defined as radar echoes coming from a region in the troposphere that contains no objects visible to even the aided eye. There is disagreement among writers concerning the cause of radar angels. Some maintain the view that the echoes are from birds, insects, or particles in the troposphere[1,2]. Although these targets will undoubtedly explain some observations, there is evidence that angel occurrence is related to meteorological phenomena as well. This claim has not been fully substantiated however, because large changes in refractive index within a few centimeters distance are required, and the presently available refractometer techniques are not capable of such resolution.

Many studies of radar angels have been performed[3], for the most part either with a weather system[9] (PPI) or a vertically-pointed, stationary beam[10, 11]. The observations on the PPI may take the form of line echoes having considerable horizontal extent, or localized dot echoes. The observations on the vertically-pointed system may be either persistent bands or coherent echoes that persist only for the order of seconds.

A third method of observation makes use of a tracking[7] radar. Roughly the procedure is to locate an echo by manually searching and then to attempt to lock-on and track it automatically. This attempt is not always successful because of the characteristics of both the tracking system and the echo. However when the echo is trackable, one can obtain information concerning its radar cross section, its motion in the atmosphere, and its "lifetime".

This report presents the characteristics of a number of angels, all having the somewhat special property of being trackable with the FPS-16 system.

# EXPERIMENTAL PROCEDURE

The track data were recorded automatically on magnetic tape and later transferred to IBM printout. These data consisted of time (usually in **10** second intervals), target range, azimuth angle, and elevation angle. In some cases, J-scope photographs were taken to record the character of the return pulse.

As a measure of power return, a record of receiver **AGC** voltage was kept. The relation between AGO voltage and power return was determined by tracking an aluminum sphere of known cross section. This relation was then used to obtain angel cross sections.

On all days when observations were attempted at least one radiosonde profile of the atmosphere was obtained. The usual procedure was to search upwind from the radar at an elevation angle of 50 degrees or higher. This increased the probability of detection since (as will be shown) the magnitude of reflection increases markedly with elevation angle. This procedure also increased the potential observation time of a particular echo, since those upwind approach and pass nearly overhead of the radar site.

# GENERAL CHARACTERISTICS

The general characteristics of the observed echoes will be given in this section. Detailed descriptions of angel behavior are found in the Appendix.

Days on which observations were attempted are listed in Table 1. This includes two clear days, four cloudy days, and two days with variable skies. On 26 March 1962 (cloudy) and 27 March 1962 (clear) it was not possible to lock-on and track a single angel. However several birds were tracked and it is interesting to compare and contrast them with angel echoes. During the cloudy morning of 30 April 1962, it was again impossible to locate a trackable angel. However, when the skies cleared at noon, a number of angels were tracked for relatively short periods of time.

On 28 May 1962, seven angels were tracked in a sensibly clear sky and three during a period of developing clouds. The onset of rain presented a cluttered picture on the A-scope and it was no longer possible to locate any trackable echoes.

On other days, the sky conditions and number tracked are as indicated in Table 1 and need no clarification.

Vertical motions will be discussed in greater detail in a 1ater.section. The figures given in Table 1 for vertical velocity are average values for each day of observation.

## TABLE I

| Sky Condition — AM / Noon / PM | 1961 | | | 1962 | | | | |
|---|---|---|---|---|---|---|---|---|
| | 12 July | 26 Mar | 27 Mar | 30 April | 28 May | 9 July | 30 July | 31 July |
| Sky Condition — AM / Noon / PM | Clear / Clear / Clear | Cloudy / Cloudy / Cloudy | Clear / Clear / Clear | Cloudy / P.Cloudy / Clear* | Clear** / Cloudy / Rain | Cloudy / Cloudy / Cloudy | Cloudy / Cloudy / Cloudy | Cloudy / Cloudy / Cloudy |
| Number Tracked | 7 | 0 | 0 | 11 | 10 | 10 | 13 | 1 |
| Average Tracking Time, Minutes | 15.7 | – | – | 2.6 | 7.5 | 9.8 | 8.9 | 6.5 |
| Number Having Upward Velocity | 5 | – | – | 2 | 5 | 4 | 6 | 1 |
| Average Upward Velocity Feet/minute | 37 | – | – | 60 | 43 | 32 | 89 | 9 |
| Number Having Downward Velocity | 2 | – | – | 9 | 8 | 2 | 9 | – |
| Average Downward Velocity Feet/minute | 129 | – | – | 190 | 56 | 116 | 63 | – |

\* All angels tracked in clear sky

\** Angels No. 1 through No. 7 tracked in clear sky, No. 8 through No. 10 in cloudy sky

7

Radiosonde profiles showing temperature and dew point as a function of altitude are shown in Figures-10-14,(see Appendix). The altitudes of the observed angel echoes are plotted here also.

Perhaps the most consistent behavior of these angels is the strong dependence of radar cross section upon elevation angle. The mean dependence for individual days is shown in Figures 1 and 2. The abscissa is the elevation angle at which the angels were observed, 90 degrees being directly overhead. Angles to the left of 90 represent an approaching target and those to the right represent a receding target.

In Figure 2, it is seen that for 28 May 1962 and 9 July 1962, the mean dependence does not behave in the same manner as that observed for other days. It is suspected that this inconsistency is due to an inoperative AGC amplifier, since the AGC voltage remained essentially constant throughout all observations on these two days. Thus the cross section data for 28 May 1962 and 9 July 1962 are probably unreliable.

Plots of some individual targets are shown in the Appendix (Figures 15-17).

Another outstanding property is the apparent coherence of the echoes. The following Figures 3 to 6 illustrate this. Each figure is a record of azimuth position error, elevation position error, receiver AGC voltage, and time.

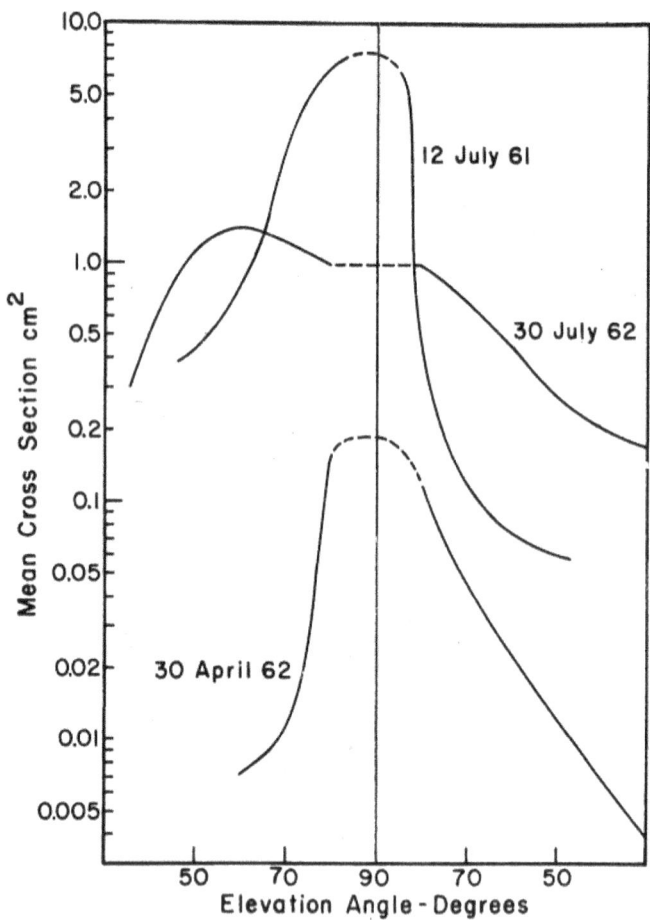

Figure 1
Mean Cross Section Versus Elevation Angle

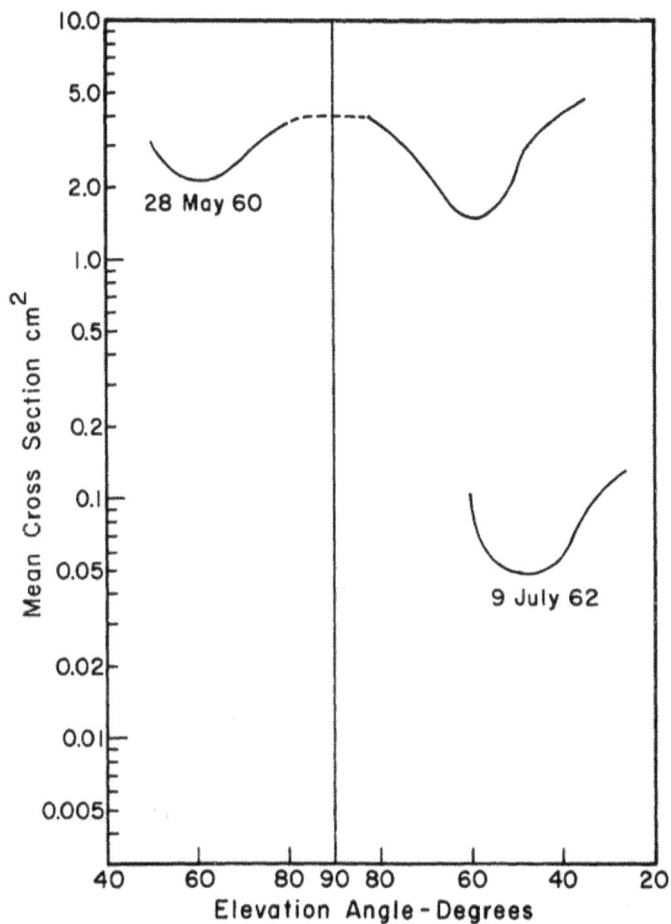

**Figure 1**
**Mean Cross Section Versus Elevation Angle**

The position error records give a qualitative indication of the degree to which the target may be distributed as opposed to an idealized point tatget. The receiver AGC voltage is a measure of the received signal strength. These records are shown for:

Figure 3 - A typical angel: range 6.6 kilofeet elevation angle 78°.
Figure 4 - The same target: range 10 kilofeet elevation angle 25°.
Figure 5 - A 6" aluminum sphere range 45 kilofeet
Figure 6 - A large bird (wing span of approximately 5 feet), range 4 kilofeet, elevation angle 10°.

From Figure 3 to Figure 4 there is a noticeable increase in the scintillation of the elevation error signal at the lower elevation angle. Angel targets cause scintillation in position error much greater than that caused by the sphere at the same range. At the same power level the angel target scintillations are usually only slightly greater, which suggests that observed angel scintillation may be attributed, for the most part, to system noise. In a few cases large amplitude scintillations occurred sporadically which suggests a target capable of becoming distributed momentarily.

The fluctuations of echo signal strength received from most angels are on the order of those from the metal sphere, and far less than those from large birds.

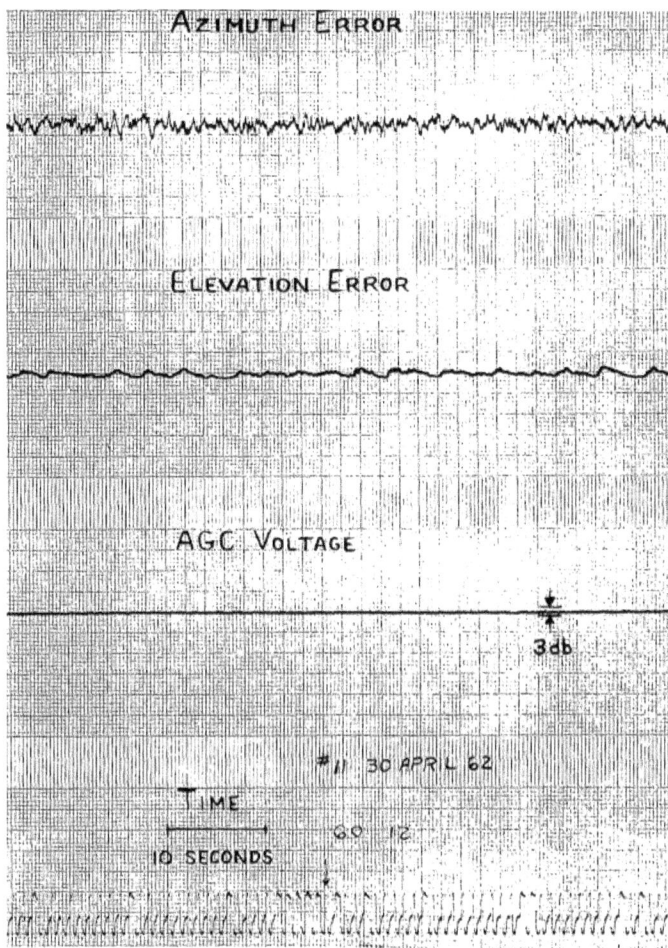

**Figure 3**
**Typical Angel : Range: 6.6 kilofeet. Elevation Angle: 78°.**

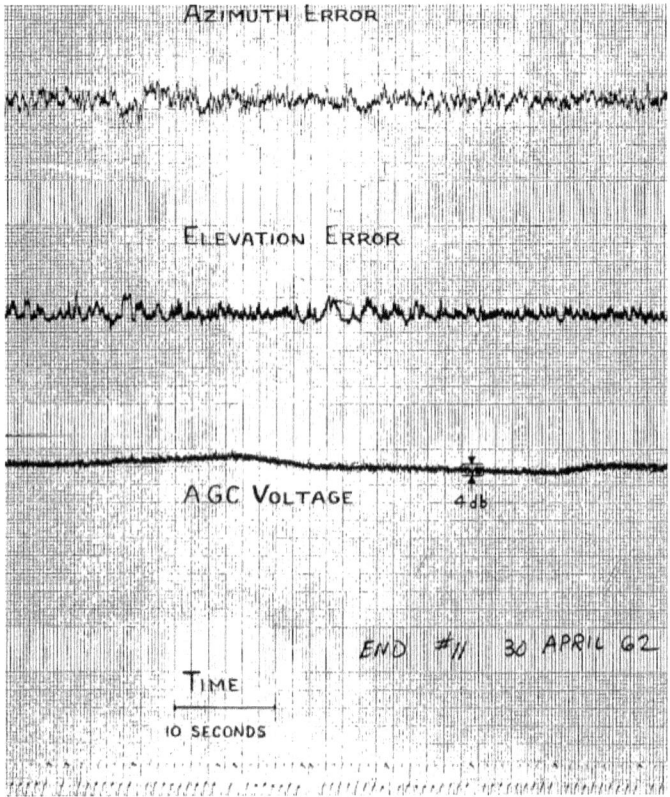

**Figure 4**
**The same target as in Figure 3. Range: 10.0 kilofeet.**
**Elevation Angle: 25°.**

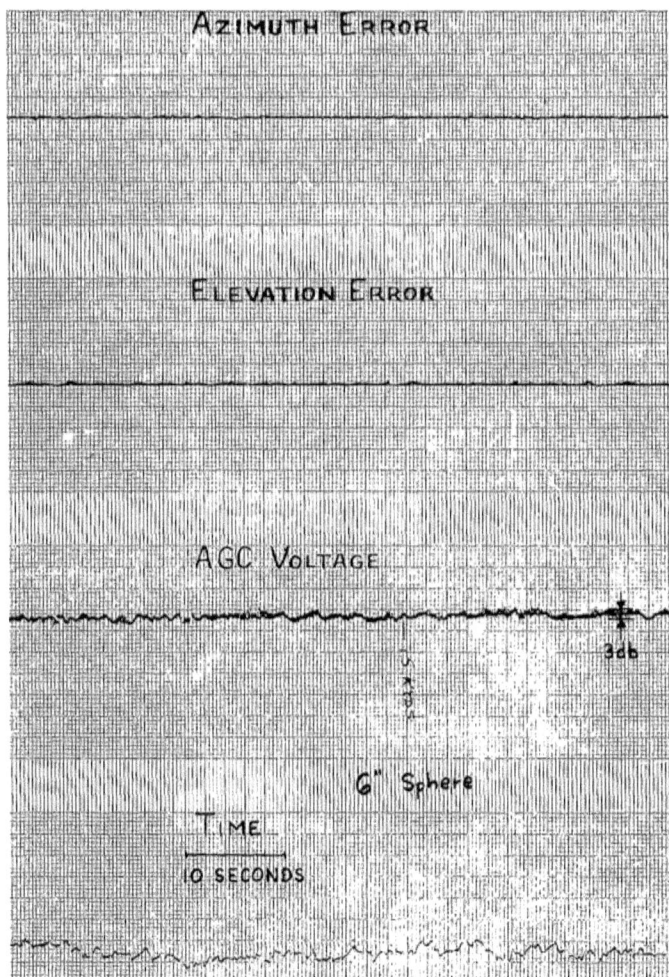

**Figure 5**
**6-inch Aluminum Sphere. Range: 45 kilofeet.**

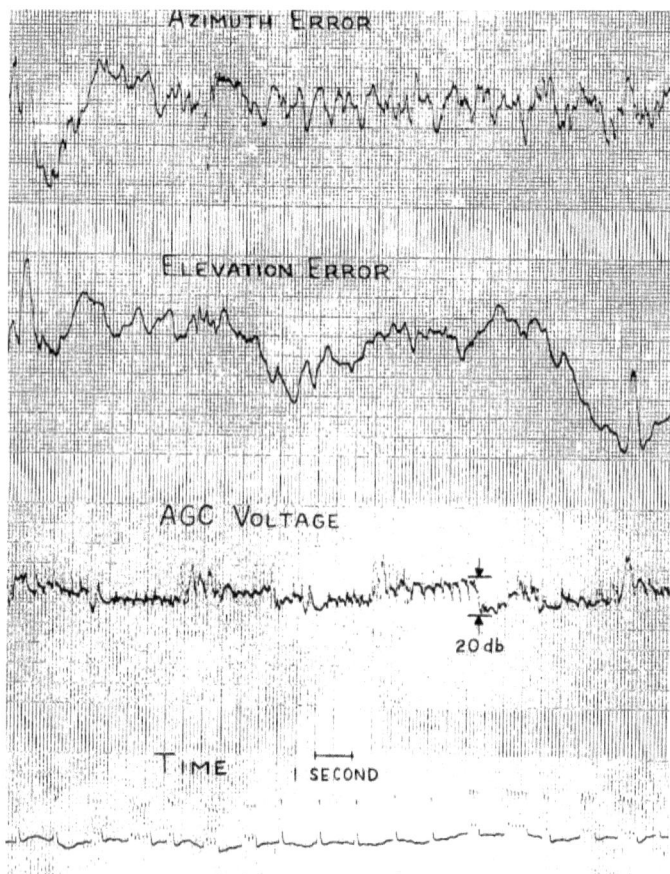

**Figure 6**
A large bird. Range: 45 kilofeet.
Elevation Angle: 10°.

Comparison of these records suggest that most of these angel echoes are caused either by very smooth layers of refractive index gradient or by a single intense discontinuity rather than by a large number of scintillating reflections. This evidence of small target size is supported by a number of J-scope photographs. Any appreciable target depth (greater than **10** meters) along the range coordinate would be detectable in these photographs. No detectable target depth was found among those investigated (about ten, over a range of elevation angles from 30 to 80°).

In Figures 18-22 (see Appendix), the horizontal velocities of a number of angels are compared with the wind velocity at the appropriate altitude. Generally, all angels observed on a particular day exhibited a consistent pattern of horizontal motion regardless of the agreement with wind data. A notable exception was found during the development of a strong sea breeze (12 July 1961, see Appendix for details). The existence of a small-scale front, indicated by the radiosonde profile, could have created winds of high variability.

In comparing angel velocities to wind velocities in the horizontal, one must keep in mind that the wind velocities are obtained by an averaging process separated in time from the angel observations by several hours. Generally, those angels tracked near the time of a radiosonde ascent showed better agreement. In some cases the angel motions showed agreement with the winds to within the measurement error of the wind data. In other cases, this error was exceeded somewhat but the time factor can explain the discrepancy.

Upon examination of many cases, one finds that angel motions have fair to good agreement with wind motions, and are highly consistent for most days. This supports strongly the notion that these angels are windborne.

Vertical Motions. The height variations of the angel sources are indicated in Figures 29-31 wherein the target heights have been plotted as functions of time. The vertical motion shows either a uniform ascent or descent or oscillations about a mean trajectory very nearly level. Often the height variations along the path are a combination of all three types mentioned above. If one considers as a unit the area within several miles of the station, and assumes that the height variations of the targets represent the vertical air motions in the region, the flow pattern obtained is not inconsistent with the existing knowledge of airflow in the vicinity of mesoscale systems. On some of the days there is a definite suggestion of a change in the flow pattern indicating the possible passage of a small-scale front characterized by different vertical air motions on the two sides of the front.

The height variations on 12 July 1961 represent such a case (see Figure 29). The angel tracks in the forenoon show an appreciable upward velocity whereas those detected in the afternoon show a downward velocity. On this particular day a shift in the direction of horizontal motion was also noticed at approximately 1100 hrs. The data immediately after this time show a well defined periodicity in the height variations with a period of 8 to **10** minutes. This has a remarkable similarity to waves of short wavelength which can conceivably occur in association with travelling disturbances such as fronts. The wavelength in this case is of the order of 2 or **3** miles.

A study of constant-level balloon flight trajectories was performed at this same location in January 1960. The vertical motions which Angell and Pack recorded have the same character as those of the angel trajectories.

Some of the constant volume balloon (tetroon) flights showed height variations of only several hundred feet over a time interval greater than one hour. Other flights showed small regular height oscillations. A few exhibited rapid large scale oscillations, with vertical velocities up to about 30 feet per second.

An air parcel rising through the atmosphere undergoes expansion which decreases its density. This increases the tendency to rise further. Similarly a downward moving air parcel undergoes compression and tends to be unstable. The constant volume balloons do not change density and would therefore be expected to exhibit vertical motions less pronounced than those of air parcels. In no cases did the angel vertical velocities exceed the largest observed value attained by the tetroon flights. Thus the oscillatory motions and occasional large vertical velocities of angels are not out of accord when compared with the atmospheric motions measured by tetroon flights.

The data on any particular day are too scant and the duration of individual records, except in a few cases, are too short to attempt a synthesis of the prevalent airflow. However there is sufficient evidence to suggest that the target path does represent the existing airflow pattern.

Correlation of Cross Section with Vertical Velocity. The average value of cross section **a** as a function of elevation angle has been plotted in Figure 1. Some targets showed significant deviations from this average value. In many cases the deviation is correlated with vertical velocity, particularly when the target is at high elevation angles. In Figures 7 and 8, the observed value of **a** divided by the average value of a (at the same elevation angle) is plotted as a function of time. In the same figure the vertical velocity of the target is represented by a dashed line. It can be seen that in these cases, the target cross section is strongly dependent upon the absolute value of vertical velocity.

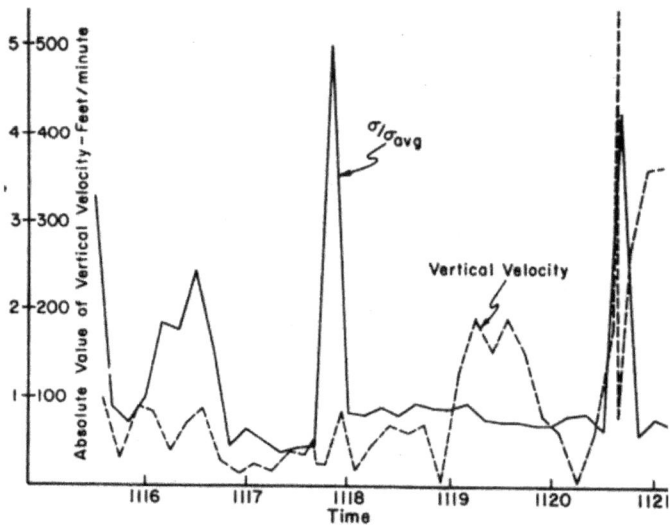

**Figure 7.Illustrating Correlation of Cross Section and
Vertical Velocity**

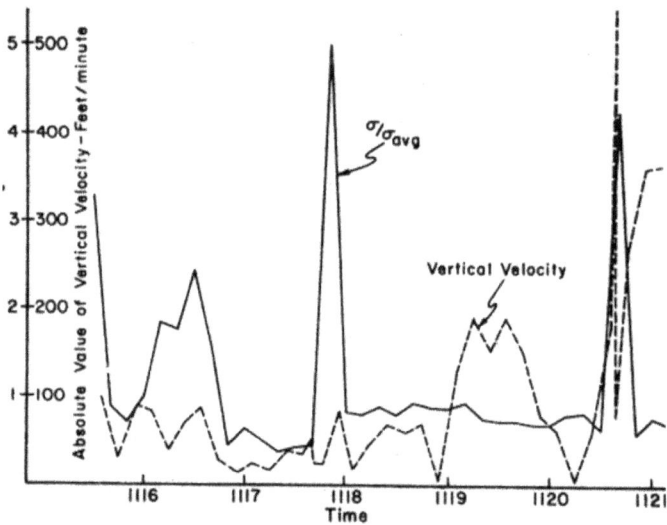

**Figure 8 7.Illustrating Correlation of Cross Section and
Vertical Velocity**

# CONCLUDING REMARKS

The preceding section contains a description of a number of trackable angels. In this section it will be shown that these angels must be meteorological rather than particulate. It should suffice to observe that the echo cannot be caused by an object imbedded in the atmosphere, but does have properties which could be explained by an appropriate meteorological model. A tentative model is suggested below.

A careful examination of the horizontal and vertical angel motions has shown that these targets are undoubtedly windborne. This completely eliminates the possibility of birds, large insects or any flying thing as an explanation for these targets. A flying target would have to show an appreciable speed relative to the wind in order to maintain altitude.

The straight-line tracks of these angels are not consistent with the flying habits of birds. Most bird trajectories are erratic both in the horizontal and the vertical[7]. . Migrating flocks might be the exception to this rule. However, one would not expect to observe migratory flights throughout the summer months and certainly not headed for the open sea.

The horizontal velocity vector of a bird is shown in Figure 20 for comparison with angel motions. The bird's velocity is significantly different both in magnitude and direction from the angel pattern and the available wind data. Furthermore, the radar cross section of the bird fluctuated regularly from 20 to 200 square centimeters - several orders of magnitude greater than the steady angel echoes. These distinguishing features make it difficult to attribute these angel echoes to birds.

The consistent, very strong dependence of target cross section upon elevation angle places stringent requirements upon the nature of any object. The targets must appear to be 30 to 100 times larger when directly overhead as compared to a "view" at 60° elevation angle. It is difficult to conceive of foreign objects in the atmosphere having this plate-like shape. It is even more difficult to imagine that such objects would invariably maintain a consistent horizontal orientation while passing over the radar station.

Horizontal refractivity stratifications in the atmosphere might be the cause of such a mirroring phenomena. Refractometer soundings indicate there frequently are irregularities in the refractive index profile. Apparently these irregularities are sometimes intense enough to create short-persistence angels, such as those observed on 26 and 27 March 1962. On one of these days, from clear skies, echoes rose sharply out of the noise on the radar A-scope; but they disappeared before automatic tracking could be established.

It is surprising to observe that some echoes persist for many minutes, and can be tracked. It may be that the more persistent angels are caused by the distortion of a horizontal refractive index stratification by a vertically moving air parcel such as a thermal. From a study of motion in and around isolated thermals, Woodward[8] has shown the distortion of an initially horizontal layer of fluid caused by the mean motions of a thermal (turbulent motions were neglected). The distortion so obtained by Woodward is shown in Figure 9.

In the region near the cap of the thermal, the layers of fluid have been intensely compacted and drawn out like rubber sheets. This would intensify existing refractivity gradients in the vertical. More realistically, the cap is a region of intense turbulence. This turbulent region may be responsible for many trackable angel echoes. The long persistence of the echo could be attributed to the long life of the large scale motion. The small intense region at the cap would account for the apprently small target size. The crowding of layers would most likely increase with increasing vertical velocity of the thermal, and this would probably increase the reflecting ability of the layers, in agreement with the observed correlation of vertical velocity and cross section.

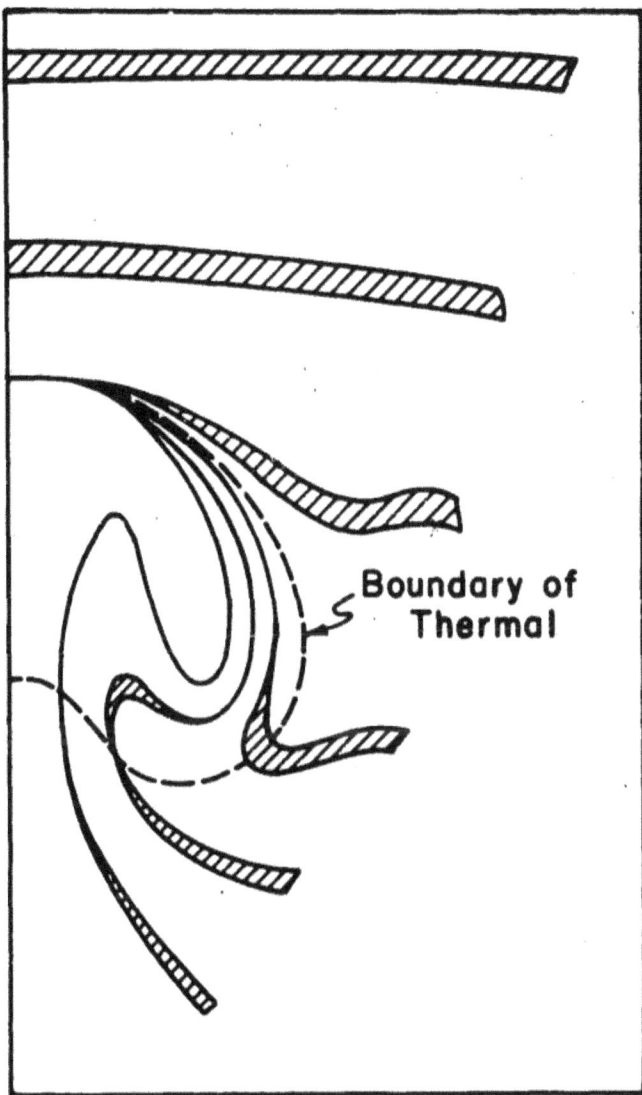

**Figure 9**
**Distortion of Initially Horizontal Layers of**
**Fluid Caused by a Thermal**

30 April 62

Angels
Winds
10 ft/sec

Time

Altitude—Kilofeet

25

# APPENDICES
## Radiosonde Profiles and Vertical Motion

In the following Figures temperature and dew point, obtained by radiosonde are plotted as a function of altitude. The vertical trajectories are shown also. It should be remembered that these are partial tracjectories indicating only that portion during which the echo was tracked.

The time of radiosonde ascent is indicated in the lower left corner of each profile. On some days two soundings were taken.

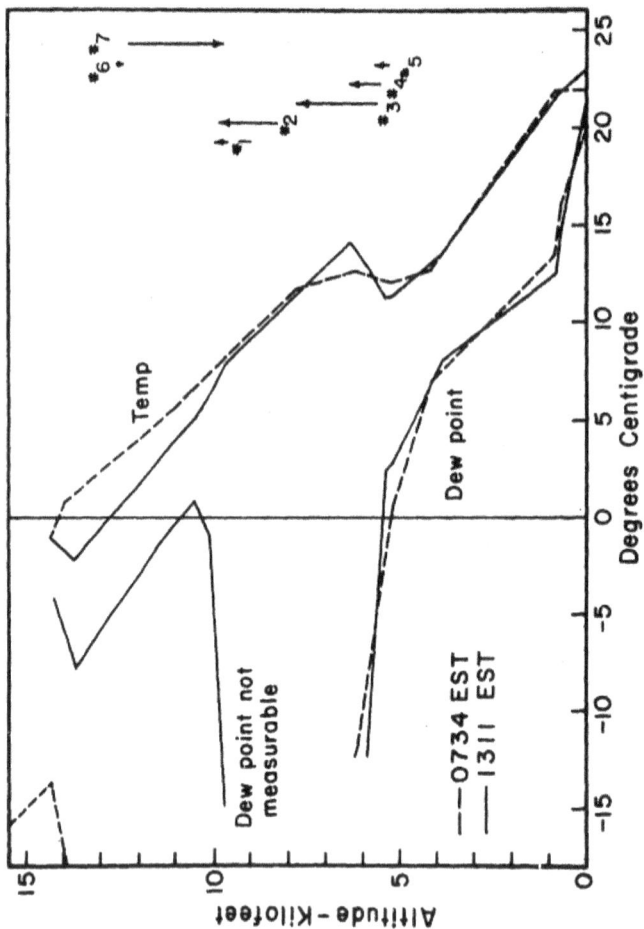

Figure .10
Radiosonde Profiles, 12 July 1961

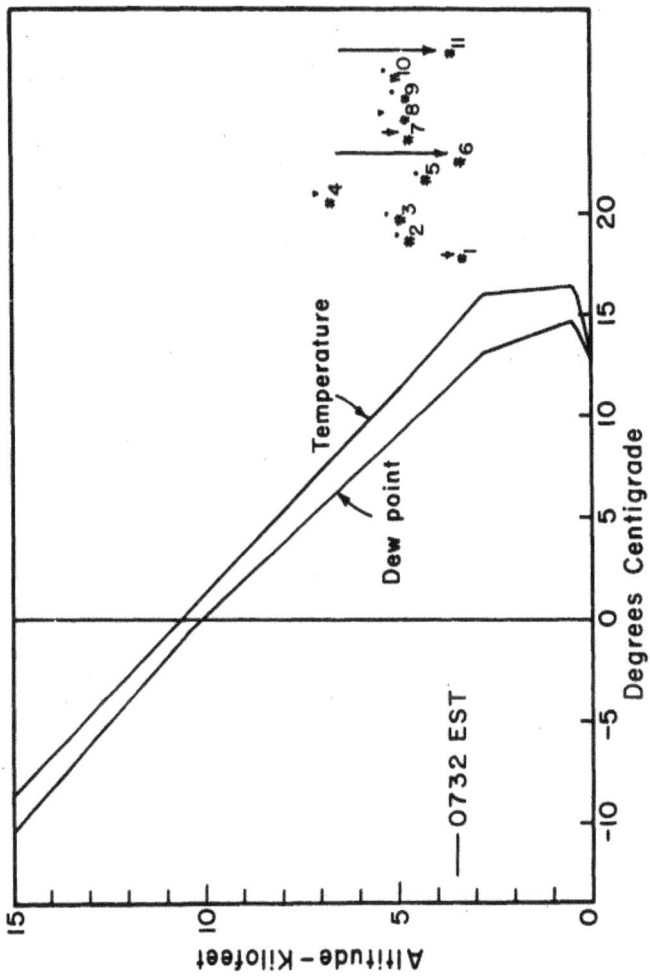

Figure 11
Radiosonde Profiles, 30 April 1962

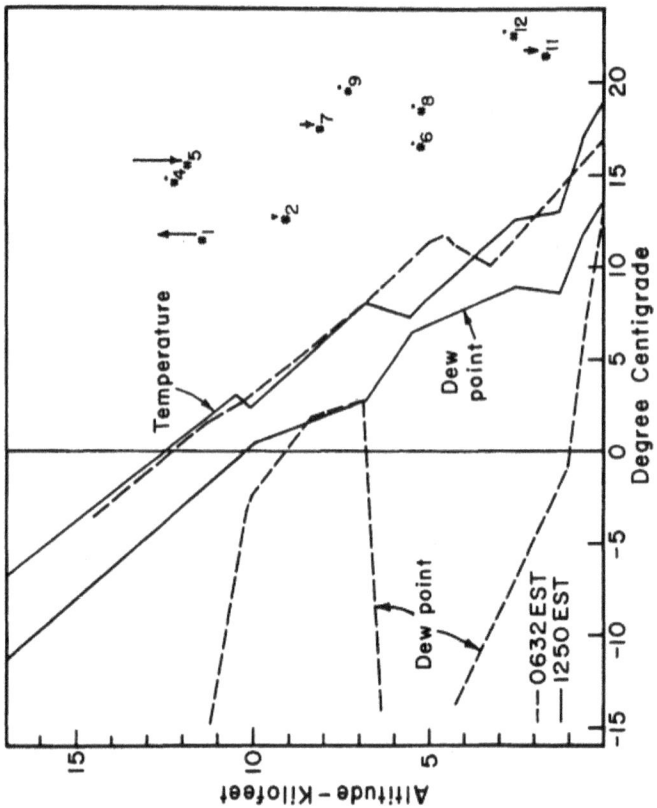

**Figure 12**
**Radiosonde Profiles, 28 May 1962**

29

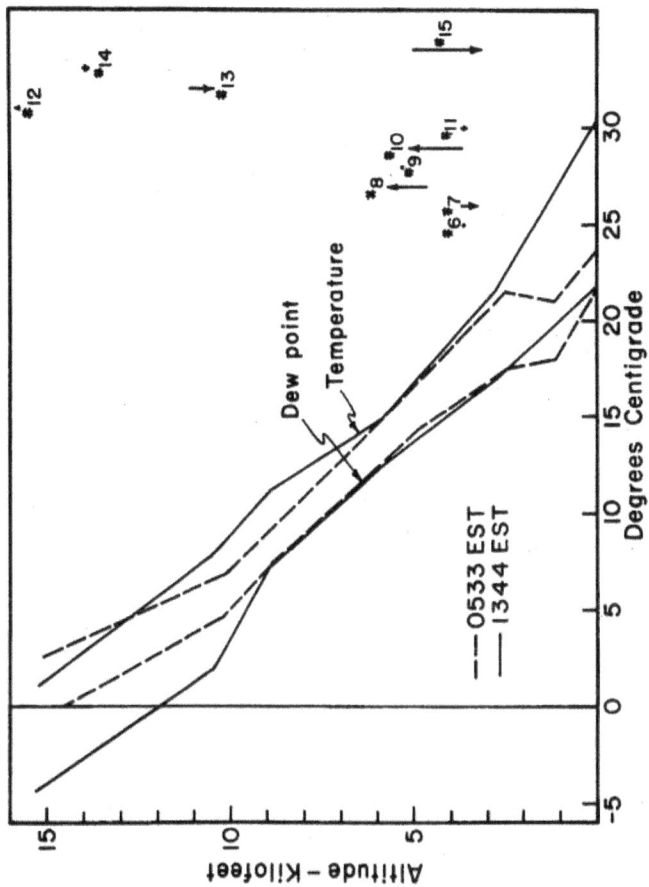

Figure 13
Radiosonde Profiles, 9 July 1962

30

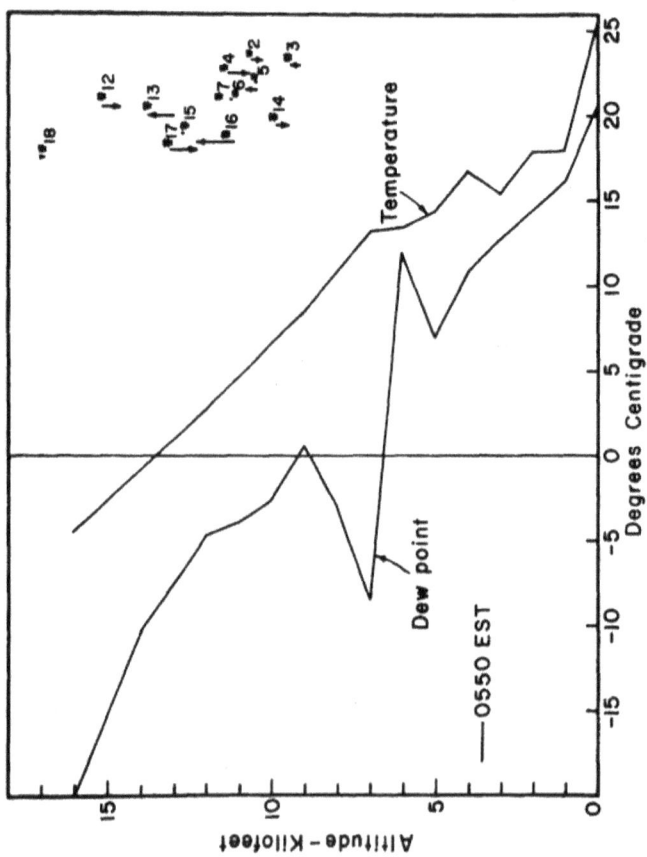

Figure 14
Radiosonde Profiles, 30 July 1962

## Radar Cross Sections

In the following Figures plots of radar cross section versus elevation angle are given for individual angels, grouped together by days.

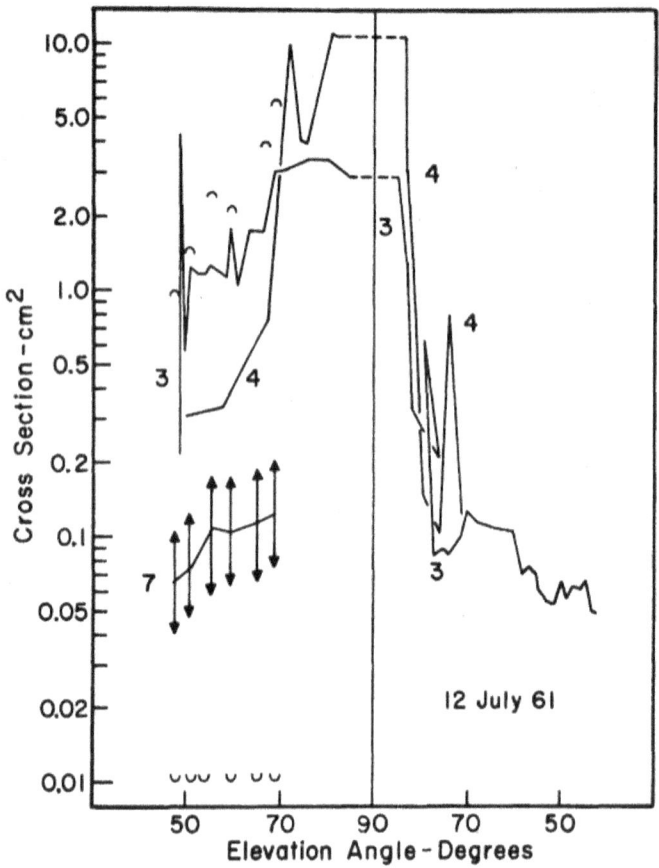

Figure 15
Cross Section Versus Elevation Angle

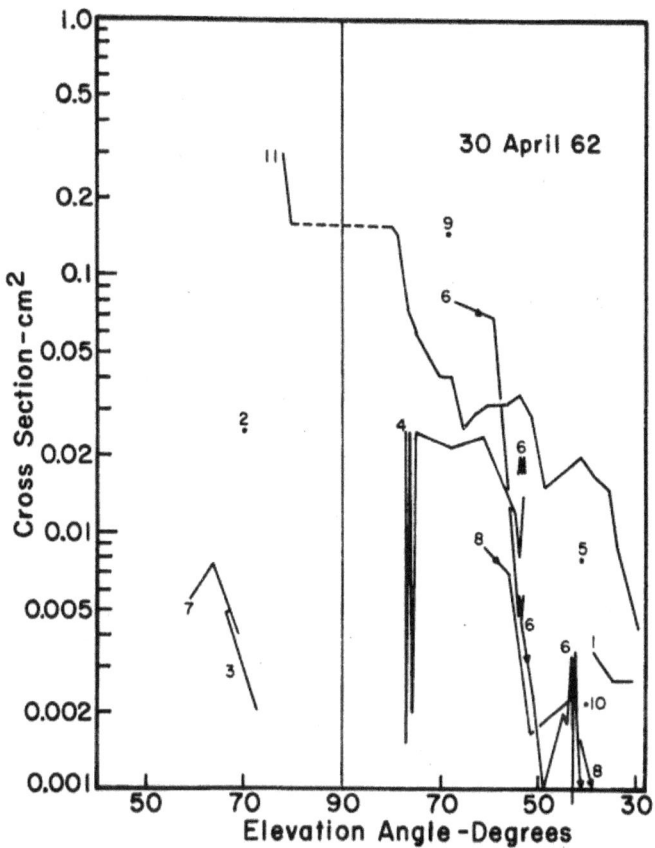

Figure 16
Cross Section Versus Elevation Angle

34

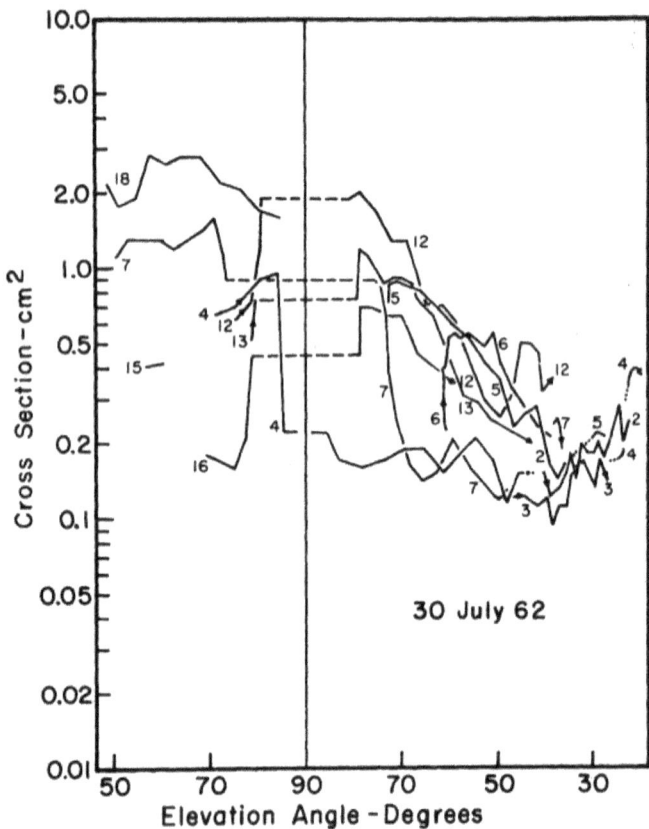

**Figure 17**
**Cross Section Versus Elevation Angle**

35

## Horizontal Motions

The following Figures compare the horizontal velocities of angels with available wind data. Each vector shown represents a horizontal velocity which was observed at the altitude indicated by the ordinate and at the time indicated by the abscissa. Solid vectors represent wind speed and direction as obtained by radiosonde. Broken arrows indicate angel speed and direction.

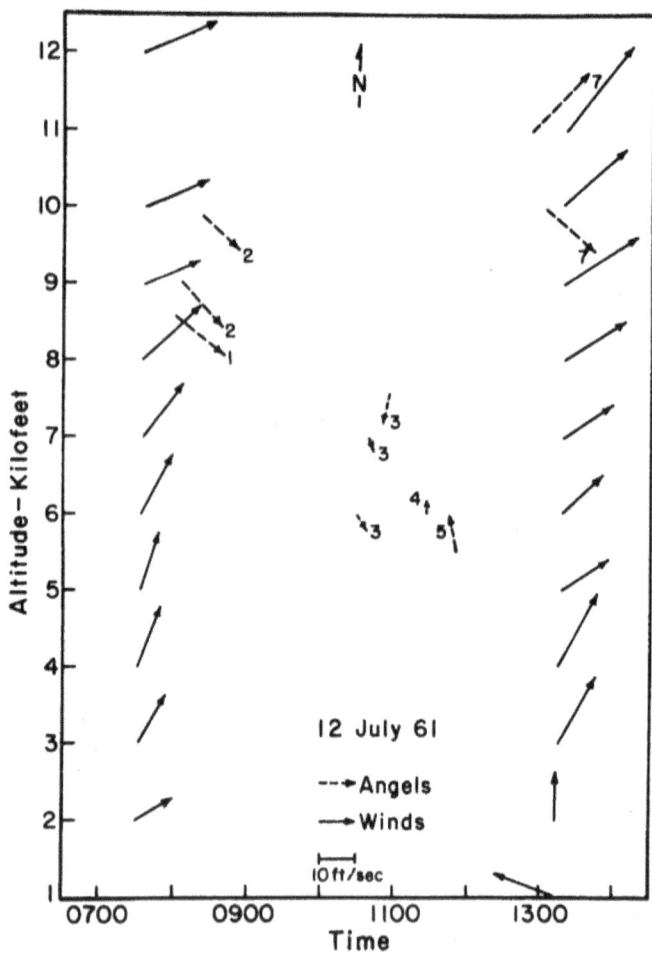

**Figure 18**
**Horizontal Velocity Vectors as Functions of**
**Altitude and Time**

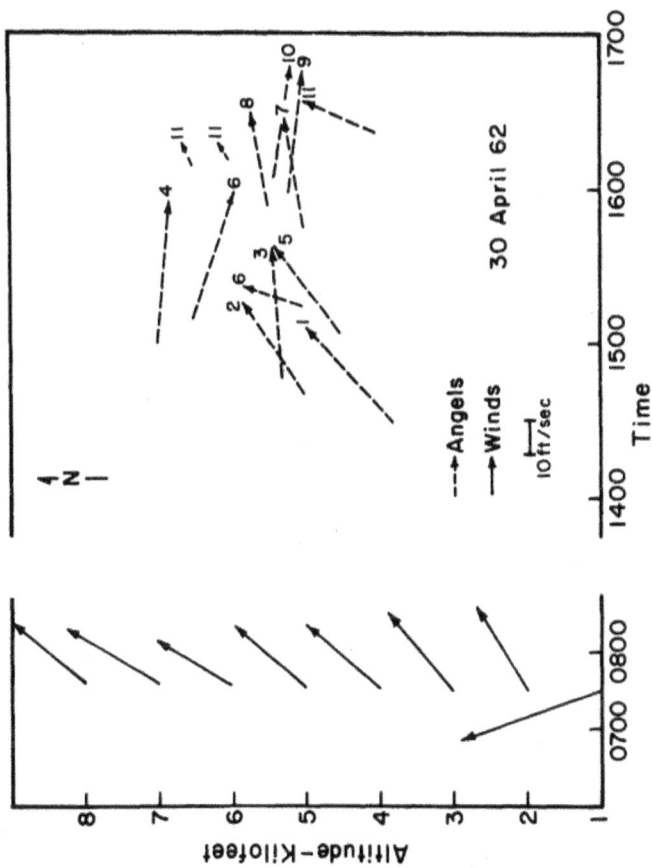

**Figure 19**
**Horizontal Velocity Vectors as Functions of**
**Altitude and Time**

38

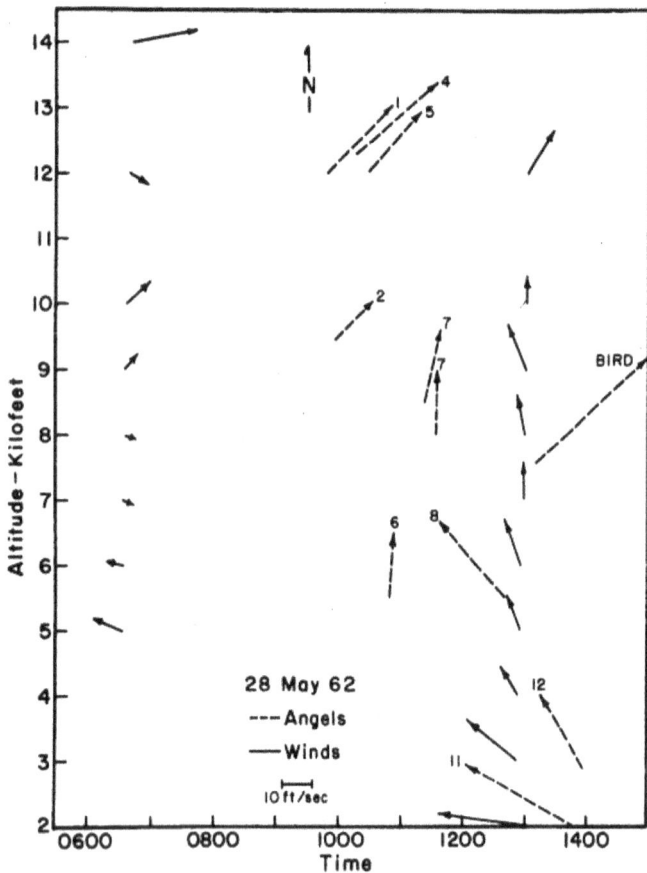

**Figure 20**
**Horizontal Velocity Vectors as Functions of**
**Altitude and Time**

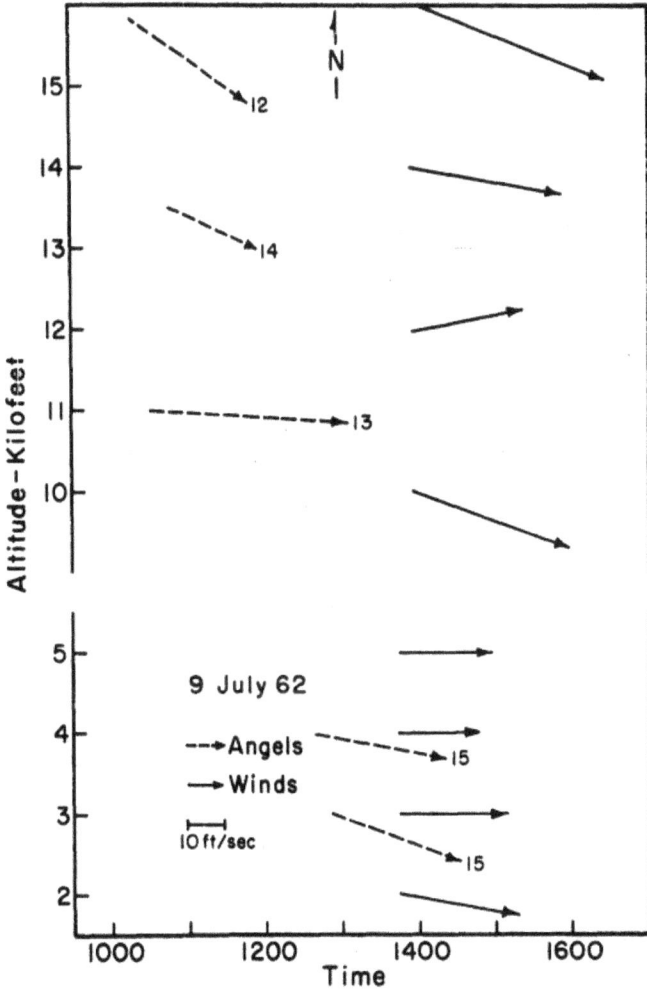

**Figure 21**
Horizontal Velocity Vectors as Functions of
Altitude and Time

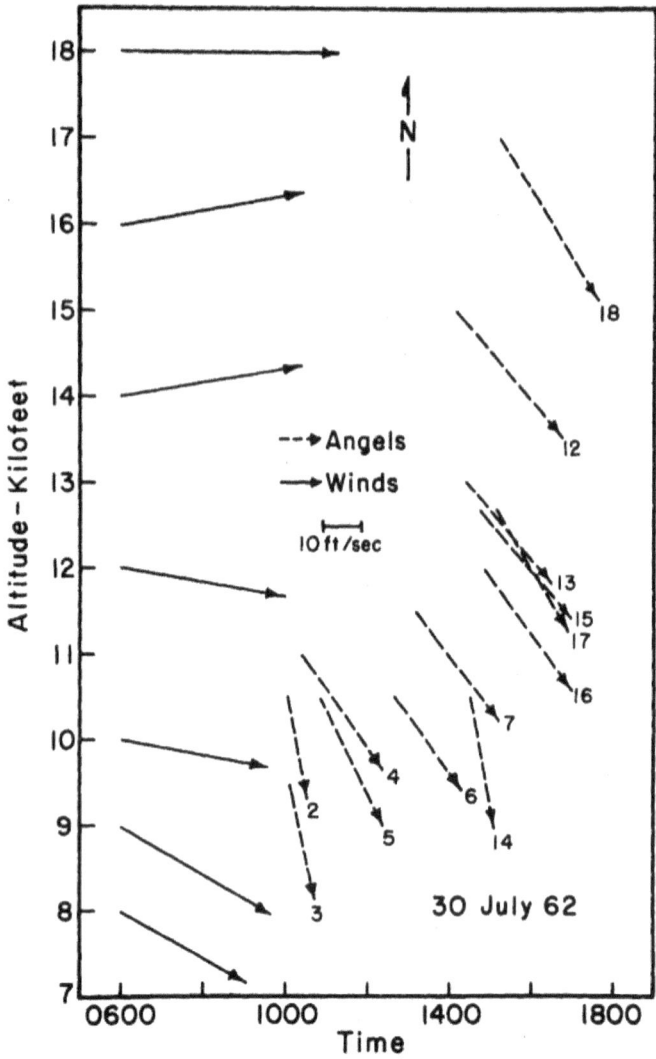

Figure 22
Horizontal Velocity Vectors as Functions of
Altitude and Time

## Horizontal Trajectories

The following Figures show the horizontal trajectories Of Angels grouped together by days. The shoreline lies at an angle of approximately 30°N and Is several hundred yards East of the radar. In Figure 25 is shown the erratic flight pattern of a bird, typical of most birds which were tracked.

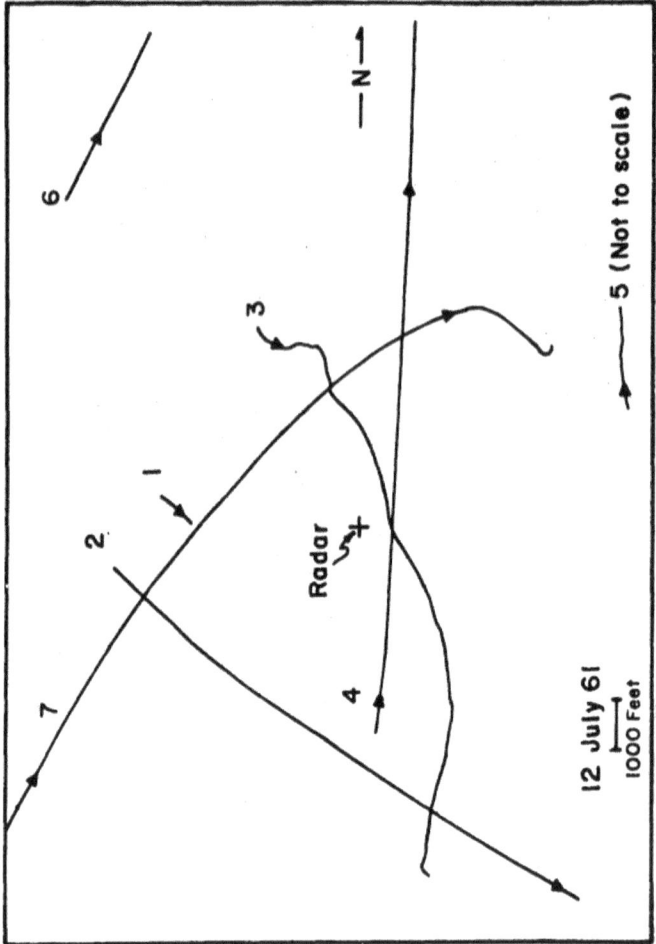

**Figure 23**
**Horizontal Trajectories**

43

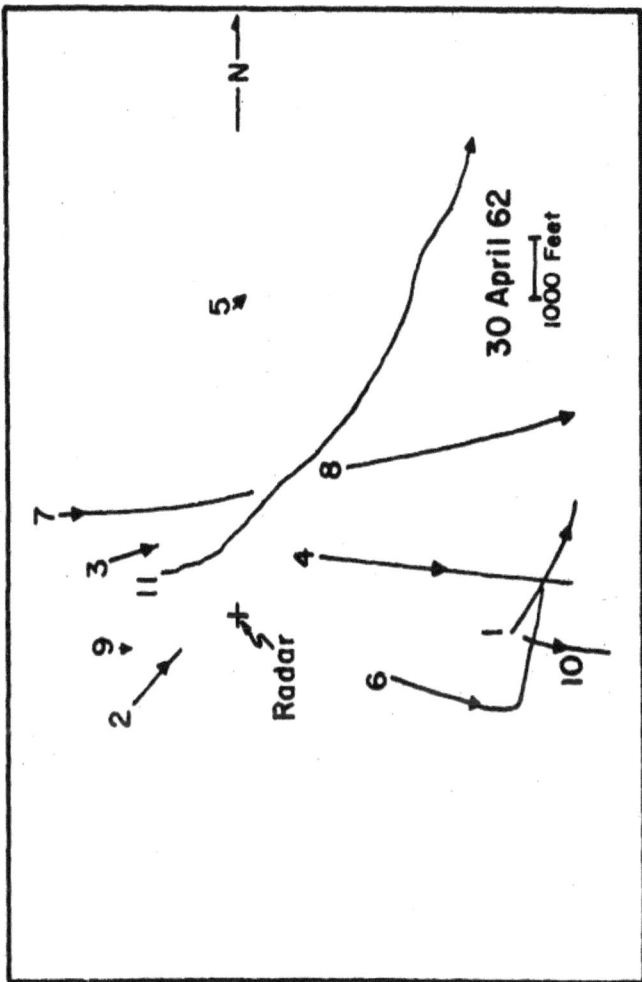

**Figure 24**
**Horizontal Trajectories**

44

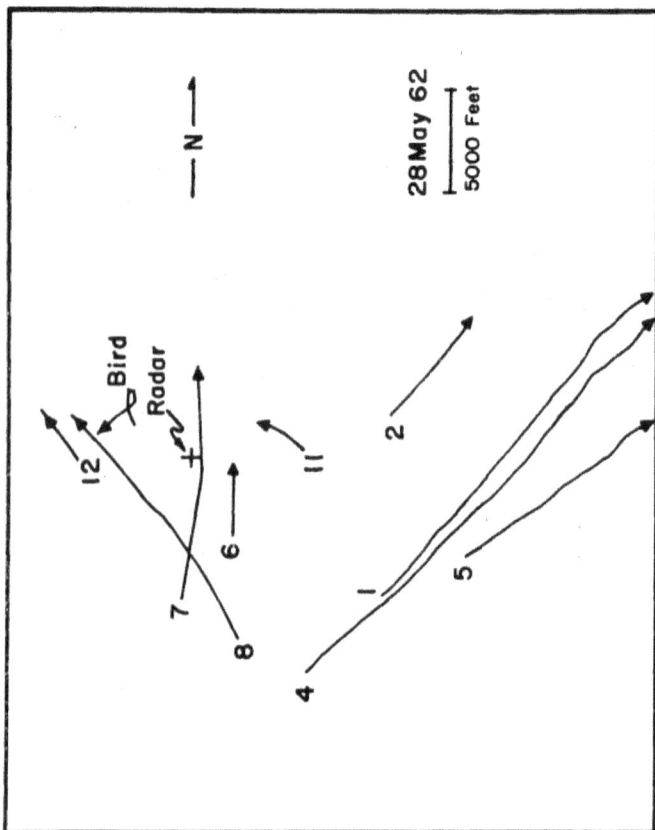

**Figure 25**
**Horizontal Trajectories**

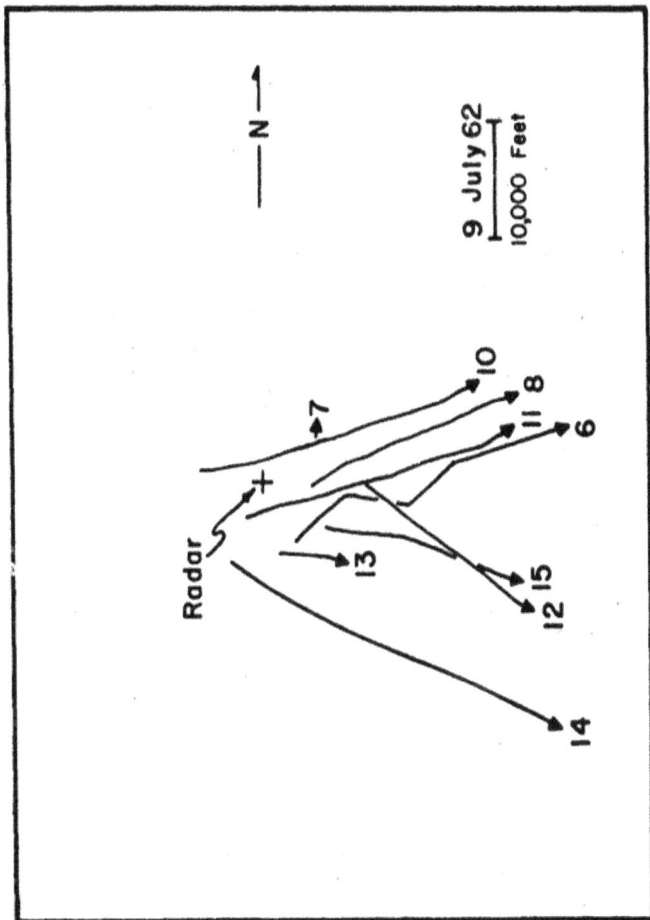

**Figure 26**
**Horizontal Trajectories**

46

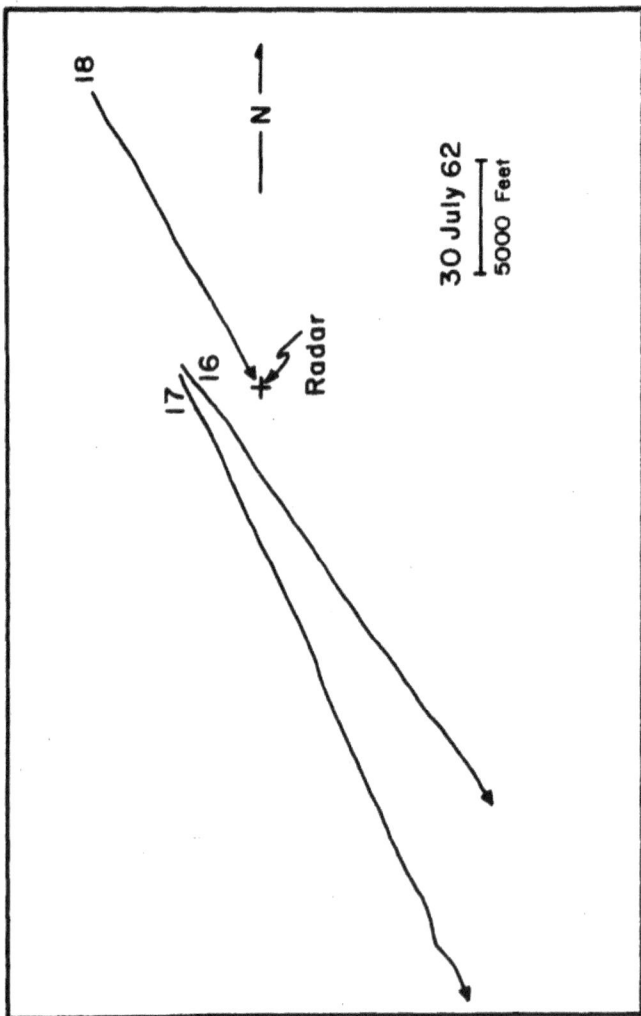

**Figure 28**
**Horizontal Trajectories**

## Vertical Motion

The following Figures are plots of angel altitude versus time for several days of observation. Note that the time scale is discontinuous so that the true spacing between angel occurrences is not represented graphically.

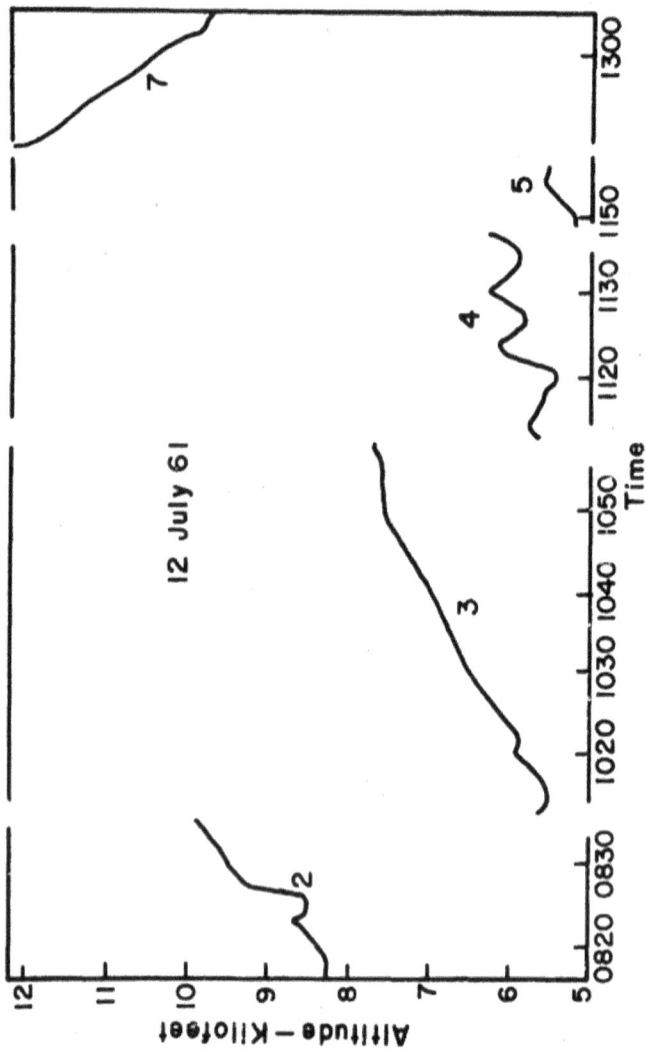

**Figure 29**
**Angel Altitude Versus Time**

49

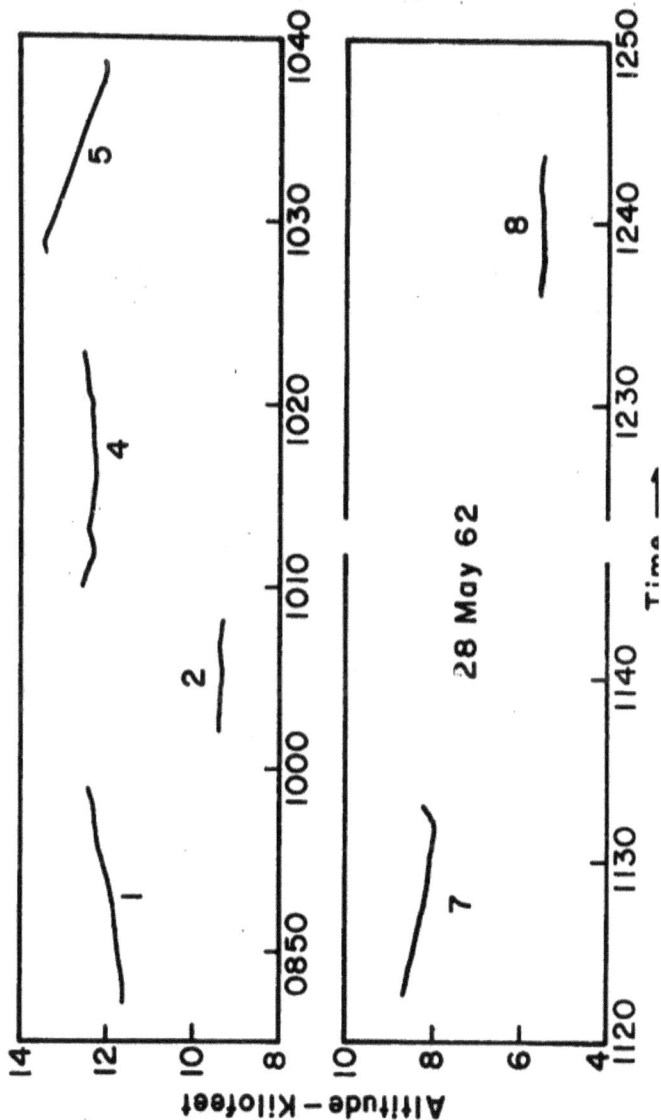

Figure 31
Angel Altitude Versus Time

# REFERENCES

1.W. G. Harper, "Angels on Centimetric Radar Caused By Birds," Nature, Oct. 1957.

2. R. E, Richardson et al., "Radar Observation of Birds," Proc. of the Seventh Weather Radar Conference, 1958.

3. V. G. Plank, "A Meteorological Study of Radar Angels," Geophysical Research Papers No. 52 Bedford,.Mass.: Air Force Cambridge Research Center, 1956.

4. R, H. Clark, "Mesostructure of Dry Cold Fronts Over Featureless Terrain," Journal of Meteorology, 18, (1961), pp. 715-735.

5. T. Fujita, "Structure and Movement of a Dry Front," Bull. Amer. Met. Soc., 3_9. (1958), pP. 576-582.

6. J. .K. Angell and D. H. Pack, "Analysis of Low-Level Constant Volume Baloon (Tetroon) Flights from Wallops Island,"t Journal of the Atmospheric Sciences, 19 (1962), pp. 87-97.

7. R..Q. Tillman, R. E. Ruskin, and M. N. Robinson, "A Study of Clear-Air Angels by Use of Horizontal and Vertical Trajectories," Proc. of the Ninth Weather Radar Conference.

8. B. Woodward, "The Motion In and Around

Isolated Thermals," <u>Quart. Jour. Royal Met. Soc.</u>, **85** (1959), pp. 144-151.

**9.** D, ,. Rai, "A Study of Radar Angels Near West Coast of India," <u>Indian Jour. Met. Geophys.</u>, 12 (1961), P. 307.

10. N. Vrana, "Some Characteristics of 'Radar Angel Echoes," Research Report RS **32,** Ithaca, New York, Cornell University Center for Radiophysics and Space Research, 1962.

11. D. R. Ray and W. M. Reid, "Radar Angels in **the** Lower Troposphere," <u>Canadian Jour. Phys.</u>, 40, (1962), pp. 128.

12. D. ,Atlas, "Possible Key to the Dilemma of Meteorological 'Angel' Echoes," <u>Jour. Met.</u>, 17 (1960).

www.ingramcontent.com/pod-product-compliance
Lightning Source LLC
Chambersburg PA
CBHW071112090426
42737CB00013B/2578